PERSONAL
ACCOUNTABILITY

A Grandfather's Plan to
Rebuild America for the Children

DON TERRY CHAFFEE
Grandfather, Former Chief Credit Officer

Printed in the United States of America by BookMasters, Inc
Ashland OH
May 2014
50004285

Rev. date: 02/28/2014

To order additional copies of this book, contact:
Xlibris LLC
1-888-795-4274
www.Xlibris.com
Orders@Xlibris.com

Dedication:

For the children... so that they may have the same opportunity and not be drowned in an ocean of debt.

Keira Anne (seven)
Timothy Baker (four)
Colin Brenner (eighteen months)
Erin Delaney (nine months)

Disclosure

I am neither a Democrat nor a Republican. I am not a member of the Tea Party. I am an Independent who does not belong to the Independent party. **I write this book as a grandfather.** *Like many Americans, I am most interested in the issues at hand. The current issues are jobs and the fact that government is not working.*

Parts of this book are excerpts from **A Return to Wisdom** *by D. Chaffee (Publish America 2009).*

Keira at 6 with an iPad

CONTENTS

PART I
We Are Accountable

Erin at 9 months

PART II
Developing a Strategic Plan for America

The Elements of a Plan

Colin does strategic planning

PART III
Let's Be Honest with Ourselves

PART IV
Becoming a More Spiritual Society

INTRODUCTION

How does one person write to the President and Congress? How do you write to other Americans? I am not sure. I think you just begin.

For the first time in my life, I am very worried about the future of our children and grandchildren. We are responsible for this situation. It was not deliberate on our part, but it was both foreseeable and preventable. We are **drowning in DEBT** at the same time we have high unemployment. **Our Government is ineffective.** It has a low rating and does not seem to be able to get anything done because everyone, all these representatives who are very good people, honestly think their way is right. Or they think they have to do it as it is the expedient thing to get themselves re-elected. This is VERY FRUSTRATING to a grandfather who refuses to believe that my grandchildren cannot have the same opportunities as my generation.

It is our mutual accountability to put America on a solid foundation. It will not be done by slogans like "cut taxes" or "cut spending." It needs to be done by the development of a **"Strategic Plan"** for our country. Some taxes need to be cut and some deductions eliminated. Some spending needs to be cut and some investments made. The budget then flows from the Plan. **Investments, not spending, need to be made in the Private Sector.** Congress does not seem to understand the difference between the two. These investments can be made by the private sector and government together. There are a variety of ways to make these investments if Government and the Private Sector, Democrats and Republicans, get on the same page. This is the only way to bring down unemployment when increased debt is no longer an option.

We can no longer accept an education system that is failing our children and everybody knows it.

What we need to do is **not that complicated.** It will be more difficult to do politically than the actual solving of the problem itself. We need to *fix the government, restore fiscal stability and grow the economy.*

Don Terry Chaffee
Grandfather

Timmy, Colin, and Keira

PART I
We Are Accountable

PERSONAL ACCOUNTABILITY

When you are accountable for something, you are responsible for it. We are all responsible for where the country is today. Not the Democrats, not the Republicans, not prior administrations, but all of us who are the citizens of the greatest experiment in democracy in the history of the world.

I believe the President, the Speaker, and the members of Congress are true Americans. In their hearts they believe passionately that they know what is best for America. The problem is that neither side has the mandate that they say. President Obama thought that he had a mandate. Then the Republicans took over the House and thought that they have a mandate. The Tea Party is sure they have the answer. In reality nobody has a mandate. Our country is split right down the middle.

To give the politicians credit, what we are facing is arguably the biggest crisis since World War II. What Americans want, taken as a whole, is constructive leadership toward a solution that is fair to all... and effective.

The true test of leadership is doing things that may not be politically popular but are the right things for our society. The American people are very intelligent. They are longing for true leadership.

We are all accountable to see that a well-thought-out plan is developed that lays a sound foundation for the future of our children. ***The bottom line is that we voted to put these people into office who cannot agree with each other.***

Please do not play with our children's future for political advantage.

I'm staring at the man in the mirror
I'm asking him to change his ways...
If you want to make the world a better place
Take a look at yourself
...and make the change

—*Michael Jackson*

THE "OSTRICH SYNDROME"

How we got here

A fundamental flaw in any democracy is that to be elected, you have to often tell the people "what they want to hear." The reason that we all are responsible is that **we did not pay attention**, for whatever reason. We were too busy just trying to manage our own lives. **Democracy seems to work best when there is a crisis of such magnitude that everyone agrees a solution is both necessary and urgent.** The best example of this would be World War II, where we definitely had to get involved and were proud of it. It does not work well when everyone is incented to "game the system" in their favor. **The result of years of gaming the system and electing politicians to maximize what we individually get has led to literally mountains of debt.** We did it to ourselves! We are accountable. We need to face this problem for our children as a matter of moral and ethical responsibility. It may be the boomers' last chance to be a great generation by putting the country on a solid financial plan for the future of our children.

Our current problems actually began a long time ago. How many of you remember Ross Perot and his warning to the nation in the 1990s? No politician in his right mind who wanted to be reelected dared to point out to the electorate the obvious. Unless serious changes were made, we were going to run out of money. Well, we have run out of money and have begun to print it at levels that have never been seen before. In fact, they do not even have to print it. They just do an electronic debit and credit, and presto, money is created right out of thin air. All of a sudden the Federal Reserve has a huge balance sheet that did not even go through the congressional budget process. Wouldn't you like to do that?

Most of us have known that social security and Medicare need restructuring for many years. Take a good look in the mirror and ask yourself, what have you done to fix the problem? Did you even really care that much?

One of the best examples of the "ostrich syndrome" is how American society dealt with the gas lines of the 1970s. As soon as the price of gas normalized, we produced more SUVs in the history of mankind. Images of Jeep Cherokees climbing plastic rocks in front of beautiful suburban homes covered our TVs throughout the day. This was precious time wasted in the development of an urgently needed energy policy. So now, some forty years later, we find ourselves still without a comprehensive energy policy with a huge dependence on people who hate us for our oil. It is a huge accident waiting to happen.

The only good news that we have is that this situation is so bad that everybody is starting to see that we have reached a crisis. Generally this is a time when we as a country can pull together and get things done.

ENOUGH BLAME TO GO AROUND

Let's take a look at those who played a role in the recent and ongoing financial crisis:

All those who used massive amounts of leverage (DEBT)

Banks who made too many risky loans

Those who distributed bad paper worldwide

The borrowers who borrowed more than they could afford

The regulators who missed it

The rating agencies who were in a conflict of interest

The investors who did not perform proper due diligence

Fannie and Freddie for encouraging it (and not following proper accounting)

A small group of AIG executives in London who blew the lid off the use of credit default swaps (CDS)

The lack of regulation of the CDS market

Americans who ran up their credit cards

Americans who used their house as an ATM machine

All those who said it was not predictable as many people predicted it

Congress and the Fed for not knowing it was happening

Once the crisis happened, the government reacted very quickly with a variety of tools that most of us thought contained the problem. In fact the pendulum has swung too far the other way with an unintended consequence of discouraging business investment in the United States.

The problem is going to get worse before it gets better. The American economy is being strangled by mountains of debt not only at the federal level, but at the municipal and personal levels as well. On top of this, the well-intended regulations that have not been written yet are a very huge burden to the businesses that we need to grow the American economy.

NOT ALL GDP IS EQUAL

Does it feel like a recovery to you?

Economic activity that is engendered by excessive debt is bogus. If you went back to the early 1990s, you would see that much of our "economic growth" has come from either debt or asset bubbles. As mentioned above, this debt is pervasive at the federal, municipal, corporate, and personal levels.

Back in the early 2000s both the Federal Reserve and Goldman Sachs started calculating MEW (mortgage equity withdrawals) in the form of home equity lines and loans and cash-out refinances. The numbers started going through the roof year after year. Keep in mind that this hard cash was being taken from a fictitious asset class because of the bubble and then directly placed into the "economy" for additions to houses, new SUVs, a family vacation, and in my own case, college tuition for my children.

On a normalized leverage basis, we are in a depression. When the government has to inject cash into the economy, and then counts the impact as real improvement in GDP, we have been hoodwinked. It's like a Monte Carlo game. At the end of the day, some of the GDP we counted never really existed.

Let me give you a hypothetical example. Let's say my daughter Meghan goes on a shopping spree and runs her credit card up to $10,000—and then defaults. Her GDP up until the time she defaulted was great, but now she has blown through her "personal debt ceiling." So she comes to her federal government, me, and explains her dilemma. Since I want to stay in her good graces and be "reelected" as her father I lend her another $10,000. Her GDP now has the ability to grow by 100% as she uses the credit card. In my way of thinking the only real bona fide GDP is that which Meghan could afford. By the way, Meghan is one of the best managers of money in our family.

When you look at the internal components of GDP, you will realize that they are all spending related: government, consumer, business, and the net of imports vs. exports. Only the private sector produces net revenue which society can then use to achieve both its basic security needs as well as higher level aspirational goals. Government spending is a user of tax revenues. All of the programs may be very worthwhile but, when taken in totality, they dramatically exceed productive capacity of the real economy. They begin to strangle that economy and may "kill the goose that lays the golden egg."

I was very surprised when the recession was declared over because there were two consecutive quarters of GDP growth. GDP is only one component of making an assessment of the economy. You cannot ignore other major factors, particularly real unemployment, counting those who have given up entirely on finding work. Thank God housing is improving as this will give us a growing tailwind over time.

Looking at GDP on an isolated basis is like only looking at the expense line in a profit and loss statement. It does not consider our aggregated national balance sheet. If you look at all of the above factors, I find it very difficult to say that we are in a recovery. Our standard of living is in decline. ***Standard of living*** is the correct measure of an economy. By that measure we are hurting. Importantly, disposable income has declined more in the recovery than in the recession!

THERE IS NO "PARADOX OF THRIFT"

GDP of 70% Consumer Spending Is Not Ideal

There is a concept in freshman economics called the "paradox of thrift." It has been bugging me for many years and I finally figured out why. There is no such paradox. The concept postulates that if consumers SAVE that they will not SPEND; thus hurting the economy. This gets at the heart of the matter that we have been discussing that GDP is the primary way we use to judge the economy and that GDP is based upon spending.

Common sense tells you that people have to save for many things: a rainy day, education, retirement, etc. If they are not doing that but spending their hard earned dollars then this also falls into the category of "fictitious GDP." Only amounts over and above a normalized savings rate are "healthy" GDP. It is not a paradox but a prescription for a stable society. People need to save. GDP generated by money that should have been saved is very problematic.

Just as important is that these savings should become investments over time. In the next chapter I will explore the difference between investments and spending. Understanding this clearly is critical to understanding the potential solution to our problem.

A GDP that is based upon Consumer spending comprising 70% of the total is frought with potential problems. It allowed the use of debt to be confused with real GDP. Consumer spending is subject to too many vagaries that leave economists and stock analysts perched on the front of their seats waiting for this month's retail sales to see what is happening to the economy. In portfolio management all of us know the importance of diversification. The same is true in managing the economy, particularly those elements of the economy that create wealth for society, and improve the standard of living for all.

WE ARE NOT IN A NEW NORMAL

We are going back to normal

Some of the brightest people in the country have suggested that we are entering what is called a "new normal." Deleveraging will cause yields to come down because you won't get the added "kick" caused by investing borrowed money. This is true. But the amount of leverage that we allowed into the system over the last 20 years was "abnormal." Allowing Banks to be leveraged at 30 or 40 to 1 was outrageous. Permitting those same institutions to engage in "Off balance sheet Special Purpose Vehicles" to hide debt bordered on criminal. It certainly cannot be considered "Safe & Sound" which is the mantra of the regulators. Any Bank that was making ROE's above 20% was taking too much risk and the earnings turned out to be losses.

We are now in the unenviable position of returning our debt levels to what would be considered "normal." This process is called "deleveraging." It has a huge effect on the economy as that debt is no longer available for spending. It also takes spending out of the economy to pay the debt.

In banking we would refer to this process as a "restructuring" or a "workout." Specialists would help the borrower determine ways to cut costs and increase revenues. **It takes both: cutting costs and increasing revenues.** Revenues cannot be increased by just raising prices because you can price yourself right out of the market. The same is true for raising taxes on those parts of the private sector that are critical to our future. **You can end up thinking you are raising revenue but in reality you are weakening your "engine of growth."**

WARNING:

EVERYBODY WANTS TO CUT EVERYBODY ELSE'S ENTITLEMENTS!

Austerity equals riots

All my life I have struggled with the question of why certain professions get paid more than others. Teachers and EMT's seem to be very important to me but society does not pay them as much as other professions. Of course teachers have summers off and hopefully get self-fulfillment from what they do. No one could pay the firemen and first responders for what they did at the World Trade Center. Policemen put their lives on the line every single day they go to work, especially in the inner cities. Doctors make good money but less than before unless they are a specialist. But they have to go through years of training. Everybody likes to pick on lawyers and Investment Bankers but the ones that do well go to the top name graduate schools and many do not make it to the top of their professions. I think professional athletes have it the best. They love what they are doing, make a ton of money, and would probably be doing it for ½ the pay! Mickey Mantle was my hero and he made $100,000 per year. Oh, how things have changed! CEO's have fallen out of favor due to the difference between their pay and that of the front line worker. Plus their pay seems to only go in one direction and is not in line with long term performance. Some CEO's have led the way to correct this and compensation committees are well aware of the outcry to change these practices. I do not know who should be paid what. But I do know that it has to be fair or the system will reach a breaking point.

If we cut too deeply, or unfairly, we may tear our social fabric. Just take a look at the food riots around the world or what happened in Greece. How long will Germany continue to save the Greeks? Or the Irish? Or the Spanish? You can envision a similar situation in the United States where more responsible states say "enough is enough."

INVESTMENTS, NOT SPENDING

When Congress hears the President talk about "Investments in the future" they immediately think "Spending." The truth is that finance thinks of them as two distinct concepts. Spending is something you do out of a revenue stream generally to support and grow that revenue stream in a given period, usually one year. One of the most fundamental objectives of a business executive is direct spending from less productive activities to those that earn a higher return. Government officials, and business executives, have a tougher job because they have to take into consideration the social contracts that have been made over time, when times were better.

Investments on the other hand generally take a longer term view. In corporate finance institutions raise money in the equity or debt markets to support the **development of new capabilities that will produce future revenue**. Generally the projects have to more then cover the cost of capital and generate a return that satisfies investors to cover the risks of the project. On the balance sheet of the institution or corporation these investments show up under long term debt or equity. Only the interest on the debt actually hits the P & L statement and is considered expense or spending. I am not suggesting that simply by reclassifying our spending our problem will go away. *What I am recommending is that we as a country, both public and private sectors, must make more investments in the private sector to generate entire new industries to lower the unemployment rate.* The government not only needs to participate in these investments, but also needs to make it easier for them to occur. The leading Investment Banks, Private Equity firms and Hedge Funds and U.S. Corporations have a significant role to play. I will go over some specific ideas later.

The most important take away is that our GDP must have a larger component of business investment, and less consumer spending.

WE NEED TO RUN THE COUNTRY MORE LIKE A BUSINESS

Although the country is not a business it has a lot of similarities. The President is the Chief Executive and the cabinet is composed of his direct reports. The Congress represents the owners. The Supreme Court makes sure we are following good governance.

The country could benefit greatly by using some of the basic principles of sound business management. The most important of these is **the development of a STRATEGIC PLAN**. The plan should not be considered central planning like the communists but a joint venture between public and private sectors. The government would lay out society goals and the private sector would talk to the consequences. The plan would have to be updated as new factors emerge.

Proper and transparent accounting is so important that I am amazed that FANNIE AND FREDDIE did not use it. You cannot hide expenses in hard to find pockets. Identification of the total liabilities is essential to coming up with a plan to either pay for them, or reduce them. Everybody in government seems to have their own set of numbers which drives all of us nuts. Accounting is the scorecard to know how well we are doing. I don't think we even know the score. Bill Gross recently mentioned our future liabilities at $100 trillion versus a GDP of $16 trillion . . . worse than Greece! The government should have to use the same accounting as everyone else. It's called GAAP.

The second area where the country could benefit from being run more like a business is performance management. Then, most importantly, people's **pay should be based upon performance**. This sounds pretty basic but when some of our best teachers are being fired because they do not have seniority something is wrong. When military parts or tools cost outlandish amounts of money, not reality based at all, we are seeing a breakdown. When everybody in our society knows that there exists outrageous waste in government and that little or nothing is being done about it we begin to look at the whole system as **a big joke**. When cabinet heads talk about the tremendous inefficiencies in their own areas **you begin to wonder who is in charge, and why is that person being paid anything?**

How long has it been since anyone has taken a look at the organizational design of federal, state, and local governments? There seems to be a lot of overlap and excess hierarchy. A good industrial engineer could have a field day.

A key part of performance management is "goal setting", `starting with the enterprise wide goals. For America *our goal is to put the country on a sound financial foundation and improve our standard of living. We need to grow revenue by having everyone's energy focused on growing the productive parts of the economy.* In business this is called "the bottom line." There are literally hundreds of metrics that are monitored monthly to monitor progress against goals. If they are missed there are consequences. In government the only consequence seems to be fear of not being re-elected if you do not bring something home to your constituents. **This actually impedes us from achieving our CORE Goals.** In many ways we actually create organizational inertia that impedes anything from being accomplished. But everyone is still getting paid, except for the unemployed who have completely given up because we have not delivered an economy that operates anywhere close to its potential.

The entire system has to be redesigned and re-engineered to be able to react much more quickly. In the fall of 2008 we entered into a serious financial crisis but we still have not taken crisp action to prevent it from happening again. Legislation that was too thick for any human to read was passed but hundreds of rules are yet to be written. **Business leaders think the unknown impact of all these rules are yet another drag on the economy. Nobody wants to invest in anything until the dust settles**. Jaime Dimon asked Bernanke "has anyone calculated the cost of all these regulations to businesses?" We still do not have a comprehensive energy policy after oil hitting all-time highs, not even to mention the gas lines of the 1970's. The oil is coming from places in turmoil. Our schools are deteriorating right in front of us with our children shooting each other. Minority teen unemployment is over 30%. There are few jobs for this year's graduates. Many are staying in school in hopes that the job market will improve. What if the jobs are not there?

We simply cannot take so long to make decisions and we need to hold leaders accountable for results.

WHY WE ARE RUNNING OUT OF TIME

Everyone seems to think that this problem is way out there in the future. Not so. Every week the U.S. Treasury sells billions upon billions of securities. Recently, China and Japan have lost their appetite. Why? Because the whole world is watching closely how we handle this situation. The Federal Reserve itself has been a large purchaser. So now the Treasury issues bonds and the Fed buys them? Think about it; one part of our government sells the debt and another part buys it!! Plus we run the risk of more asset bubbles. Some in Congress are looking at more stimulus. Again the thought is to put money into the economy not realizing that the only thing that goes up in real terms is debt.

Every day people look at the news and see what is happening to Greece, Spain, Ireland and Portugal. They then hear our leaders, at high levels, talk about actually letting our government default if only for a few days. It seems that they are looking at this as an "opportunity" to advance their particular agenda.

If investors do not show up to buy our securities one day, because there are just too many of them, the last financial crisis will look like a walk in the park. If the dollar loses its status as a reserve currency its value will decrease significantly.

Our elected officials are playing with nitroglycerin. So far we have been very lucky.

IF YOU KICK THE CAN, PUT A DENT IN IT!

Kicking the can down the road can be helpful... **if you put a significant dent in the can.** Sometimes, in order to buy time, people come up with a temporary solution that is better than the crisis. Each and every time they do this, it is important to make the potential crisis smaller.

WHAT DO WE HAVE GOING FOR US?

A lot! Do not bet against America. We are tenacious, innovative, and want to work hard to get ahead. America is still the greatest economy in the world. I think it is the greatest country in the world and count my blessings that I was born here. It has the potential to remain a powerful engine of growth that the entire world needs.

All we have to do to restore the world's confidence is a demonstration that we are willing to face our problems. We do not even need to make immediate drastic cuts that would lead to social upheaval. All we need to do is to have a **REASONABLE PLAN.** *The plan needs to unleash the power of capitalism, properly regulated, and harness that power to grow our economy to its full potential.*

We also should tell the world soon that we will not ever default on our debt.

WHY CHINA WILL NEVER SURPASS THE U.S.?

The proper way to measure a country, and the effectiveness of its economy, is based upon its standard of living, including the rights and freedoms it provides to the citizenry. Even if you just look at GDP, you should look at it on a per capita basis. The individual's ability to get ahead based upon hard work is a very powerful motivator.

PART II
Developing a Strategic Plan for America

THE ELEMENTS OF A PLAN

Vision Statement
The Environment
The Mission
Priorities
Outside-the-Box Ideas

VISION STATEMENT

One person cannot write a vision statement for a country. What I can do is put forward some ideas as to what would be included.

Why Does America Exist?

American democracy exists because of the bravery of a small group of pilgrims who could take no more and left everything behind in search of a better future for their families. The vision was to replace tyranny with freedom. The price of this freedom was high: a long journey, loss of lives, hard labor, and finally, a revolution against the King of England where the American revolutionary army sacrificed everything and David slew Goliath.

These hardy pilgrims became the foundation for the spirit of American independence and ***our fierce commitment to the Bill of Rights,*** and a somewhat suspicious view of government that, left unmonitored, may produce unintended consequences, even with good intentions. The blood of generations has been spilled to protect our way of life. America exists because we will fight to the death to protect our way of life.

When government no longer meets the needs of the people, at the most fundamental level, it begins to crack at its foundation. The fall of the Soviet Union is a great example. The communist centralized economic system stymied individual opportunity and suffocated from within the hopes and aspirations of its people. President Reagan recognized this long ago and exploited the opportunity and changed the course of history.

Currently, the U.S. government has ***lost the trust and confidence of the people.*** Trust and confidence have to be earned over time. The election of a Democrat, or Republican, who promises change, is meaningless unless behaviors change and the American people start to see a cooperative spirit that begins to take us in a direction that actually deals with our great challenges, the solution to which will create the world for our grandchildren.

So the **first element of our statement** is:

> **A government that works.**

This is probably asking a little much. Let me be clear. This is not to say that we agree with the government. What it means is that our representatives start to cooperate and work in constructive ways to do what is best for all the people—not just saying what they need to get re-elected. At a minimum they need ***to stop shouting at each other.*** Campaign finance reform and term limits need to be seriously considered to "take the money out of politics."

The **second element** would be:

Fiscal stability is restored.

We cannot go on spending money that we do not have just to show GDP growth. It is essential that we do this in a manner that is a **fair deal**—no sector of the society should win out over the others. The idea is to "grow the pie" so that all benefit. There will be sacrifices that have to be made, but they should be shared and not draconian in nature. Social security and Medicare need to be saved, but changes have to be made. People who have made tremendous sums of money need to have their benefits reduced. People are going to have to save more themselves and take better care of themselves or they will have to pay higher premiums.

The **third element** is:

The American dream remains alive and well.

"The land of opportunity" has always been our credo. If you worked hard, you get ahead. A good education led to a brighter future. Growing the private sector is the key to providing the jobs that will enable this dream to continue to exist.

Next:

Terrorism is contained.

I think it is naïve to think that given the forces of evil in the world, and the history of the world, that we can rid ourselves of the scourge of terror. It seems to be caused by a minority of extremists. I think the most we can hope for is through proactive intelligence and covert operations that we can minimize the terrorist's ability to do us harm.

Finally:

Our children must have the opportunity to get the best education in the world.

Something awful has happened to our educational system over the last forty years. To me it is a real embarrassment. We have gone from one of the best in the world to one that is mediocre. In some inner cities it borders on horrible. I do not think the answer is to throw more money at it. The answer is personal accountability by all the constituents. We will spend a chapter on education later.

These elements represent, in my opinion, the core of a vision statement; a government that works, fiscal responsibility without social unrest, the restoration of the American dream, controlling terrorism, and a good education.

It Must be a Fair Deal
Rich, Poor, and Middle

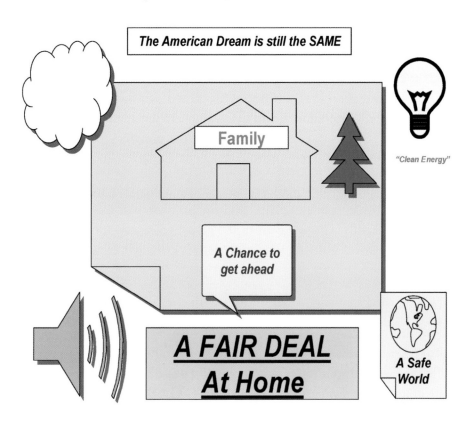

THE ENVIRONMENT FACING US

The environment is treacherous. The recent HBO movie "Too Big to Fail" based upon the book by Andrew Sorkin laid out how close we came to the total collapse of the financial system. Unfortunately most Americans are not aware of how interdependent these institutions are and how quickly confidence can turn to fear. Money and capital markets can literally "freeze." Very strong companies lost their ability to finance their daily operations. Money market accounts that invest in what is usually considered safe short term obligations found they were illiquid.

Many Americans screamed out "just let them fail," not knowing that the Lehman failure could soon be followed by AIG, Fannie and Freddie, Merrill Lynch, Morgan Stanley, Goldman, Wachovia, Citi, and then the other big banks. Although, in a normal environment, many of these were solvent, the freezing of the flow of funding would bring them all down. The result would have been **Great Depression II.**

The world is drowning in debt.

The parents of the boomer generation were petrified of the great depression. They feared debt. The boomers learned the tax benefit of debt. Generation X and Y feel they are "entitled." As mentioned earlier a lot of economic growth of the last 20 years was really counting debt as growth.

As we speak the probability of default in Greece is at an all-time high. Spain, Portugal and Ireland are not far behind. The Euro may implode when the Germans get tired of paying for other countries' excesses. If this happens, the European banks take a big "hit" and the problem will reach our shores. The European economy will be affected and this will put a dent in the global economy. All of this may not happen, but the risk is higher than ever before. Whether the Greek debt is extended or not, the losses in that debt are real right now.

The government is confusing quantity of regulation with the "effectiveness of regulation."

To be fair if you were sitting in congress and saw how close we came to the edge, you would want to act aggressively as well. The problem is that the pendulum is moving dramatically to the other extreme and is beginning to stifle the eventual solution: growing the private sector. Let me give you just one example. After the fall of Enron, the Congress passed "SARBANES-OXLEY", one of the most onerous and costly bills that was supposed to make sure that internal controls and executive accountability that would prevent such occurrences in the future. It did not work. In fact, I think it made matters much worse. People became deluded that we had thousands of little controls that had to be signed off on by thousands of executives that had to be reviewed by thousands of auditors. It simply did not work and it caused us to take our eye off the ball of what was happening right before our eyes—**the growth of asset and debt bubbles.** Unfortunately both of these bubbles burst at the same time while literally thousands of executives were signing off that their controls were just fine. The bottom line is that Sarbanes-Oxley did nothing to prevent the financial crisis.

The Tax Code is Killing Us.

If you want to grow jobs you have to encourage investments that will **create jobs for Americans.** Congress does not want to even address the tax code now. They say it is too complicated. Probably they mean it is too political. It is too important not to address now. Whatever we do, it has to be perceived as fair. The code has to be dramatically simplified; loopholes eliminated, and in *the process support the growth of jobs.* In my opinion some taxes have to be lowered, and some increased. Warren Buffet admits that he should pay more than his secretary! Since most of his income comes from capital gains and dividends he pays a low rate. That is what anyone would do in his situation. Very wealthy Americans should pay more than the 17% that was recently reported in the Wall Street journal. The Corporate tax rate, meaning **actual taxes paid,** needs to be in line or better than our competition. This would be somewhere between 23 percent to 25 percent. New businesses that grow jobs that are in future important industries should get a *significant break. Think about it. Companies that create jobs in America deserve a tax incentive.* By turning unemployed workers into taxpaying citizens the program will pay for itself and create a higher standard of living for all.

Our competition is becoming ferocious.

In the second half of the twentieth century America dominated the world. The military industrial complex after WWII kept us well in the lead. Now the tables have turned. The Chinese have the ability to replicate almost any item at a tremendous cost advantage. India has become a major focal point for outsourcing of American jobs particularly in the technology arena. In this case they have a low cost of labor and a plethora of young people who have been educated in the best schools in the United States, and anxious to get ahead. Japan is making moves to get their economy back on track. Remember, we want the capital in America to build our future and create new industries and jobs. **We will not make it unless the government becomes supportive of business, large and small.**

The Middle East is literally on fire. A new World Order is forming.

The volatility in the region is at an all-time high. Protestors are being shot by their own governments. Although democracy may make inroads there is no assurance that new democratic governments will be friendly to the United States. More than ever we need to have an energy policy that leads to independence.

How can we not have an energy policy?

Super-civilizations are replacing super powers. Borders are less relevant. It is much better to grow the global pie than it is to try to take a piece of another's.

Terrorism, despite Bin Laden's death, remains alive and well.

The killing of this mass murderer was a victory for the United States and our special forces. President Obama deserves credit as well. We know from history that terrorism is like a cancer and we need to treat it like cancer with monitoring and targeted radiation. I talk about fighting terrorism in a later chapter.

Our education system is failing our children

Over the last 50 years we have gone from the best to "mediocrity." We are not even giving people the right skills for the jobs that are currently available. As I have said before this is not a problem that we can fix by "throwing more money at it." If we don't get education back on track we will not be able to compete in the new global economy.

Summary Of The Environment

My conclusion on the environment facing us is that we certainly have our work cut out for us. I remain convinced that we still will be the greatest country in the world... if we work together. If we divide each other we will increase the eventual pain that we will all suffer.

OUR MISSION

Our mission is to re-engineer the American economy to harness the power of the private sector. The healthier the private sector is the more we can spend on social programs. Our goal is to bring us close to our full economic potential, minimize unemployment and raise the standard of living for all. Our core challenge is to attract capital and investments in activities **that create jobs in America.** To achieve this mission we must cut some spending, raise some taxes WHILE CUTTING OTHERS and eliminate ineffective regulation. All entitlements need to be reviewed and prioritized against each other by the American citizenry. Someone has to be put in charge of eliminating waste, wherever it exists. We need to restructure education and agree on a national energy policy. The Tax Code needs to incent investment in American jobs. Our ratio of debt/GDP must return to acceptable levels. We need to do all of this without causing social upheaval. IT CAN BE DONE.

GOALS
"A Grandfather's Plan"

AKA: Jobs, Jobs, Jobs

1. **Fix the Government**—DO NOT IGNORE THE FACT THAT OUR GOVERNMENT DOES NOT WORK.

2. **Restore Fiscal Stability**—A 15 YEAR "STEP DOWN DEBT GROWTH PLAN"
   Grow the Economy
   Trim Spending
   The Tax Code must incent jobs
   Regulations Streamlined but with Serious Consequences

3. **Agree on an Energy Policy**

4. **Accountability in Education**

5. **Contain Terrorism**

6. **Become a more Spiritual Society**

Has anyone else noticed that jobs have fallen from the headlines?

HOW DO WE FIX THE GOVERNMENT?

Let's not make the "ostrich syndrome" mistake again. Our government is not working. We, the citizens, need to get it to work. Here are a few suggestions.

1. TAKE THE MONEY OUT OF POLITICS

A major flaw in democracy is that politicians tell people want they need to hear to get re-elected. In fact in our system they have to say one thing to get their party's nomination, and then move to the middle to get elected nationally. Massive amounts of money flow in from unions, wealthy donors, corporations and in the last election, grass roots internet contributions. Politicians say that these contributions do not influence them. Do they think we are stupid?

Again, campaign finance reform is an issue that has if asked, most Americans would say "absolutely." It has been debated for 10 years but no politician wants to do it out of fear that they may lose more than the other side! So nothing gets done.

It is time to address this issue. Votes should not be able to be bought and sold, whether directly or indirectly.

2. TERM LIMITS SHOULD BE CONSIDERED

The great advantage of term limits is that elected officials no longer say and do things just to perpetuate their time in office. You also eliminate the "old boy network" that develops over time and leads to seeking and returning favors.

3. CONGRESSIONAL PROCESSES ARE OUTDATED

Have you noticed that we wait until the very last minute to make very important decisions? Take for example the debate on the debt ceiling or the recent debacle on the payroll tax. And, at the end, the decision was not made. **At the end of the day we are stuck in one big filibuster. Did you know that our elected officials often do not even go the filibuster. They just play music?**

Some of the processes and procedures in Congress go back over a hundred years and are meant for a different era. In business we would call this managing the "workflow." Regularly we would review it to do things more efficiently or design technology to handle them. There has to be a way to force issues to a head, debate the critical elements, write the bill in easy to understand English, and have an up or down vote. So much of the time spent now is posturing for political advantage.

Then the results should be reviewed to see if things are working as planned. For example, Sarbanes-Oxley is very expensive and cumbersome but it certainly did not prevent either the financial debacle or all the fraud that is part of it.

4. THE SINGLE MOST IMPORTANT THING WE NEED TO DO TO FIX THE GOVERNMENT

We must vote for people who put the interests of our entire country above those of their own personal self-interests.

BEGIN THE PROCESS OF RESTORING FISCAL STABILITY

We need to put America back on a sound financial footing. Everybody agrees. However they seem to want others to take the pain. We cannot keep America great unless we all share the pain to free up investment money for the future. In order to do this we have to cut some spending and raise some taxes. *We need to be very sensitive as we do this to attempt to not already harm a weak economy.* But we must keep in mind that one of the reasons the economy is so weak is the massive debt load that is weighing us down. Investors see that as a major impediment for investment. It represents massive potential future taxation which causes them to look to other places to invest.

We only have to begin the process in a serious way to show the world that we are acting in a financially responsible way. Attempting to cut $1.2 trillion over 10 years did not meet that test. Ultimately the effort failed because one more time highly intelligent and good people failed to compromise. In order to have any chance at achieving financial stability we must do three things:

1. Begin to trim entitlements in the fairest way possible and do it slowly. There is no magic to 10 years. It is much more important that the Plan is credible. 15 YEARS GIVES US MORE TIME TO ADJUST.

2. Introduce a tax code that **stimulates investment in jobs in America.**

3. The economy has to grow or we won't make it which means we need a "growth strategy."

The challenge is tougher than we think because the current forecast has overly optimistic GDP projections and allows for no recession nor the possibility of a foreign war.

HOW TO TRIM ENTITLEMENTS IN THE FAIREST WAY

The two main programs that have served us very well for many years are social security and Medicare.

Social Security Reform

Simply put there is not enough money to keep the program as it was originally designed. The basic intent of the program was to provide a "safety net" for people. At age 10 my father died of a massive heart attack and my mother looked forward to that social security check every month to help pay for the very basics. I am very grateful for the program.

If we have to cut back most experts think we need to move out the date individuals receive and "WEALTH test" the participants. If a person takes advantage of all our country has to offer, goes to college, works hard, succeeds in a career and is able to retire early with significant wealth, then their benefits should be lower. They will argue that the money is theirs. I would argue that the money was a term insurance policy that protected them very well.

We will have many debates, and arguments, about what amount of money is "significant"? My own opinion is an estate above $3 million should start to receive 75%, $4 million 50%, $5million and above 0%.

The younger generation feels absolutely abandoned by this program. They are paying for something they feel 100% sure will not be there for them. To them it is like someone is stealing their money. It really is just a tax. I do not know if they are right if we make the above reforms. ***However, I think younger people should be given higher IRA and 401K benefits to help them save for retirement.***

Medicare Reform

Medicare has been a terrific program that has helped millions of people over the years. It is very difficult to reform it as it involves making changes that literally have "life and death" consequences. It is a political nightmare to tell a person that their benefits are going to be cut. So how do we save it?

First, I think people have to be clearly told that the program is insolvent, that there will be **no Medicare** if changes are not made. *We also must provide enough lead time so that current recipients do not lose vital services.* To begin with the same two steps that were taken in the social security recommendation above need to be done to Medicare:

1. WEALTH testing
2. Give people choices
3. Motivate healthy habits

Some people want to be "fully insured" and are willing to pay more money in premiums over the course of their lives. Others want to not have to pay these higher premiums and prefer to have the government not take their money. 40% of expenses occur in the last year of life and are mostly for very expensive chemotherapy treatments and high cost operations. For that type of benefit people will have to have a choice, and if they chose it they will have to pay more.

We also need to *change motivation.* People who live unhealthy lifestyles need to pay more.

Unfortunately, **Obama Care will have to be amended.** The country simply does not have the means to pay for it. It has also become *a serious impediment to job creation.*

Finally *tort reform has to be implemented.* The great American lawsuit boondoggle has to be reined in. The attorney lobby has been so strong that his has not happened. The result is liability insurance has driven costs upward and some health fields are no longer economically viable.

HOW TO GROW JOBS

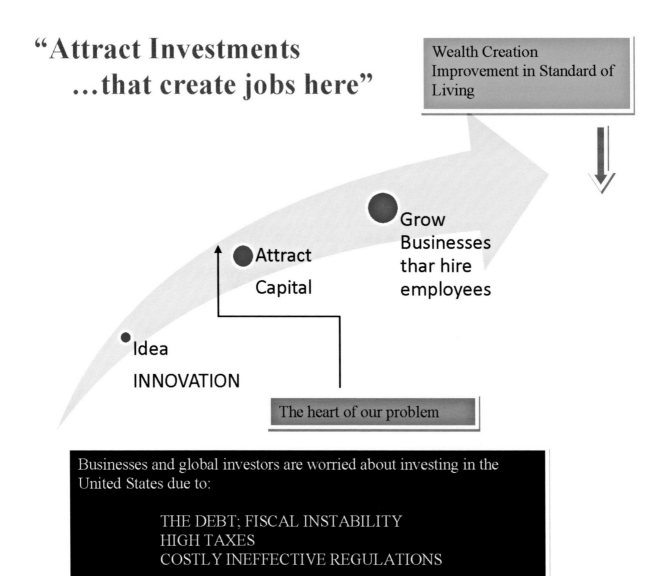

"Attract Investments ...that create jobs here"

Wealth Creation Improvement in Standard of Living

● Grow Businesses thar hire employees

↑ ● Attract Capital

● Idea
INNOVATION

The heart of our problem

Businesses and global investors are worried about investing in the United States due to:

THE DEBT; FISCAL INSTABILITY
HIGH TAXES
COSTLY INEFFECTIVE REGULATIONS

What caused this system to break down?

EXCESSES

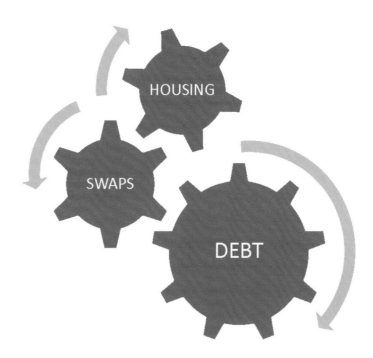

It truly was "irrational exuberance" to quote Alan Greenspan. Only he did not realize that it was not just the tech bubble. Debt was becoming pervasive throughout society. In the old business cycle it was a buildup of inventory that eventually led to a recession. ***This time it was the end of a business cycle, the crash in housing and the debt bubble bursting all at the same time.*** This is a major problem for us because housing and debt have been major drivers of our economy. Once the gears stop, as the markets froze after Lehman, it creates a fear and inertia that leads to lethargy. ***Something needs to be injected into the system to start the engine of capitalism… and it cannot be debt.***

HOW DO WE "RESTART" THE ENGINE OF OUR ECONOMY?

There is only one way: *make America a great place to invest and to locate jobs.* To do this we must undo all of the issues noted above.

1. Government needs to be much more supportive of business. It is now viewed as the "enemy." WE CANNOT COMPETE WITH CHINA THIS WAY.
2. The Debt problem has to be addressed. It is scaring off investment.
3. The tax code must incent GROWTH AND INVESTMENT in American jobs.
4. Regulations have to be streamlined but with consequences.
5. We need a plan for housing and energy.

Americans need to understand the importance of the Private Sector in generating the revenue that pays for all of our programs. THE PRIVATE SECTOR IS MOSTLY SMALL BUSINESSES. It needs to be nurtured. It also needs to be properly regulated and the regulations must have teeth. The global competition we are facing demands a more cooperative spirit between government and the private sector.

We are wary of large corporations. This, in part, has been caused by the poor behavior of a few. That poor behavior hit the headlines in a big way. There is also tremendous anger at the large compensation packages that have not been linked to performance. CEO pay is out of line as a multiple of front line workers. Boards of Directors are now "on" to these issues and beginning to address them. It will take a while for large corporations to regain the trust of the average American. Our challenge is to incent these large companies to invest the cash on their balance sheets in job producing activities here at home. Give them a benefit to repatriate foreign investments and put it to work in America.

THE TAX CODE IS KILLING US

Recommendation: The Step Down Debt Growth Plan

It took 20 years to get into this problem so it probably will take 15 years to fix.

Reduce the deficit each year by 1/12 for 12 years by cutting spending and raising revenues in those areas that hurt the economy the least. Investments that create jobs in America should be significantly tax advantaged. The new jobs that are created will more than pay for themselves in new tax revenues and the "multiplier effect" will increase "good spending" in the economy as these new job holders buy things. We should continue the program to reduce the debt with a goal of debt to GDP of 90%. As long as we hit the targets the debt ceiling would be auto approved. If we do not that year's proposed deficit would be closed by reducing spending by 60% of the amount and raising revenues by 40% or the new debt ceiling does not get auto approved. It is a shame that we have to hold the debt ceiling over our heads but it is necessary.

Everyone keeps saying that that the tax code changes must be "revenue neutral." That would be a huge mistake. They need to GROW THE ECONOMY and to produce a lot more revenue!

I was very impressed with the work of the Simpson Bowles committee and the open and honest disagreements they had. At the end they came up with a recommendation that most people, democrats and republicans, think has merit. The plan lowers rates, eliminates loopholes and broadens the base. Everybody has to pay some taxes.

I think the plan should be enhanced to provide tax credits for investments that are directly linked to creating jobs in America. **For example, repatriating overseas profits should get a huge tax credit if invested in US jobs.**

We are all taught in freshman economics that fiscal policy should be used as one tool to nurture the economy. We need to turn the tax code from a negative to a positive. Providing tax incentives to grow jobs and the economy is critical to the goal of restoring fiscal stability.

At the end of the day I think there is a good chance to accomplish some form of this objective because eventually we will be forced to do it. It would be less painful if we could start sooner. One of the best things President Obama has done was to set up this Blue Ribbon group of highly credible bipartisan individuals. One of the worst things was to ignore them.

Not all loopholes should be eliminated. They should be reviewed using only one criterion: do they create more jobs and thus tax revenue than they cost in lost revenue from the deduction itself. The best example is the residential mortgage deduction which I think should stay in place for loans up to $500,000 but phased out over 5 years for higher amounts (or at least reduced).

Capping the loopholes seems to be the easiest and fastest and fairest way to get this done.

ENERGY

Implement a national energy policy that frees us of foreign oil. Any day there could be a war in the Middle East. Get the "buy in" of corporate America as to the best way... and do it. Start with the Boone Pickens Plan and add to it. ***Building infrastructure for gas trucks, electric cars, wind and solar could be new industries that are major sources of job creation.***

"Project Independence"

*When a young John Kennedy stood up and told the nation we would go to the moon by the end of the decade it inspired a nation. We need to rid ourselves of our dependence as fast as possible. Call it **"Project Independence".** **I am convinced that not only can we do it but it would be a way for all Americans to share in fighting the war on terror.** We need the President and the new Congress to make it happen. It will take a lot of people working together: the oil companies, the auto companies, the utilities, the farmers, new entrepreneurs and the American people. Key to making it happen is to make it advantageous to all---the use of capitalism tied together with protecting mother earth. There is a huge new market out there that should provide attractive returns to early adopters. Taking your destiny into your own hands reduces not only our enemy's opportunity to use this tool against us, but gets everyone involved in solving the problem.*

EDUCATION

"F"

Over the last 50 years we took the best and made it mediocre. We have thrown a lot of money at it. We have done a lot of studies. But at the end of the day the results are horrible. There are some excellent schools throughout the country. The top 10% of the students hold up pretty well. But it is unbelievable to me that we are graduating students from high school that really should be graduating from the 8th grade.

At the New Haven Savings Bank we made a loan to a new charter school named *Amistad Academy.* In my mind it is **The Model.** A young woman named Dacia Toll, a Yale law school graduate, gave up a lucrative law career to start the school. The bank provided the loan to purchase a building in a very poor part of town and Dacia did all of the rest.

Students and parents had to apply.

This made it clear that there was a certain type of student that would be accepted: one that was committed to getting a good education. **Just as important was that the** parents had to be actively involved in the **program. Education is A FAMILY AFFAIR.**

The application process also showed the world that it was very prestigious to get accepted into Amistad Academy.

Teachers were carefully selected for their skills and PASSION.

I never saw a group of people who were so dedicated to the CHILDREN. When you walked around the hallways there was a contagious enthusiasm. Smiles were on everyone's faces. There really was learning going on and being enjoyed. People got raises and promotions based upon performance. Unions were not needed because people were happy.

Have you ever wondered how in our public schools the young new teachers start out very altruistic but within 10 years become disenchanted? Many of my friends in the 60's went into teaching for the long vacations and great benefits. Not the best reasons. They have told me that eventually the "administration and bureaucracy" sucked whatever passion they had out of them. In the inner cities the kids were wild, violence was prevalent and the parents were nowhere to be found.

Administration was kept to the minimum.

The goal here is to get the dollars into programs that train the kids. In America there are way too many school districts with massive overlaps. Again we have to follow the business practice of moving nonproductive expenses into excellent teachers and programs.

Discipline and a dress code were enforced.

No boys walking around with their pants down so much that their underwear is hanging out! Everybody understood that it was a privilege to go to this school. They have pride in their school. If you did not actively participate in the program there was a long list of kids who wanted to replace you.

School days went to 5 PM with mandatory activities and plenty of public speaking.

Learning to participate in groups and on teams is critical to life success. Public speaking is something most adults fear. The more you do it the less you fear it. Doing public speaking well is a real advantage.

There is plenty of extra help.

This school does not wait for you to have problems. They monitor students closely and address issues early. If your daily work was not up to par they do not wait for a report card!

The Results: OUTSTANDING GRADES & KIDS

Every local politician now wants to be on the Board of the school

EDUCATION PRIVATE SECTOR COORDINATION

It is **terrible testimony to our lack of a plan** that there are 3 million open jobs in America but people do not have the skills to fill them. The evolving private sector needs to have much more direct input into the education system so the kids are much more aware of where the jobs in the future will be. If we don't do this the jobs will be outside the United States. I am not saying that we force our children into the future jobs. I am saying they need to have the information to make better decisions.

Many large companies have their own "universities" to train employees. In the future we may want to have some students go directly to these programs to help for a better connection to the business world.

I am a big believer in a liberal education having gone to Georgetown. I do not want to lose all of the elements of the "renaissance man." However, we have to be much more pragmatic if we are to compete in the global economy.

With regard to the 3 million jobs mentioned above I hope the government will work closely with these companies to do on the job training to employ as many as possible. This is a real shame.

OUTSIDE THE BOX IDEAS

#1
BUY STOCK IN AMERICA

The United States has a fundamental capital structure problem that any first year finance student would recognize. Our Balance Sheet has all debt and NO EQUITY. It has never been done before but WHY CAN'T THE US GOVERNMENT ISSUE STOCK??? If we can issue all this debt why not stock?

Some of you, who are as old as me, may remember how popular U.S. Savings Bonds were extremely popular to pay for WWII. I used to get them regularly as a child from my grandmother. However, a bond is DEBT, and it carries an interest rate.

There are HUGE advantages to issuing stock. Unlike a debt obligation it does not have to be repaid at a fixed maturity date. It may or may not pay a small dividend that could be tax free with no capital gains tax. This program would more than pay for itself, particularly in a rising interest rate environment. The Stock could be issued at $10 so all Americans could participate. The stock would then trade in the secondary market and its price should improve as we improve our fiscal stability and the economy. The most important benefit of stock is to:

Pay Down the Debt

The simple step of replacing debt with stock would immediately improve the deficit and our cash flow as a country. There would be less debt needed to be issued to pay for maturing debt in a rising interest rate environment.

This is a much better idea than raising taxes because Americans would have a decent chance to make a return on their money, and directly participate in turning the country around.

This idea is one where the Investment Banks could really help out by underwriting the stock and distributing it.

#2
HOUSING

"Turn Housing into a Job Creator"
by
Turning the Secondary Market Back ON

Fix Fannie & Freddie

It is time to fix FANNIE & FREDDIE. I find it unbelievable that we have neglected this for such a long time. Ideally you would like to have a secondary market that is unfettered by the government but this may take 5 years. You absolutely need a well-functioning secondary market to shrink the Federal Reserve's balance sheet to more normal levels. We also need to do this to reduce and stop the bleeding sooner rather than later.

How do you do this?

1. Take one of the agencies and make it the ongoing core of the secondary market. It should be owned by the industry and 20% by the government for 5 years. Keep the government guarantee for 5 years as the housing market recovers. Eliminate subprime but allow 10% down for new home buyers with good credit. Mortgage insurance should cover the other 10%.

By having the Banks own the Agency you reduce the "moral hazard" of pushing bad paper to the "greater fool."

2. Take the other agency and make it the Asset Recovery Bank. This agency would have all of the problem loans and REO. This agency should be owned by the top 20 Banks based upon their pro-rata share of the bad loans and 10% by the government. This bank should operate similarly to the Asset Resolution Corp after the last debacle. It's mission is to put itself out of business as soon as possible while achieving acceptable but not ideal returns. Private equity should be able to invest on a

"tax free" basis to incent demand, and limit the use of federal money to solve the problem. The longer we wait the more it bleeds!

#3
THE ELECTRIC GRID IS MORE COMPLETE THAN YOU THINK

Why not have a national program to have a solar roof on every building and house over the next 20 years?

Take out of work residential construction workers, add a tax credit to the home owner, make it a national high profile program and bingo you have a significant part of our energy independence goal. The money saved on unemployment and the tax revenue generated would pay for the program. The capital budgets that utility companies currently need to spend could also have huge savings.

Dow Chemical has now developed a shingle with the solar cells built right into the shingle. The residential contractors who are currently out of work could do the job. This would be a massive project and could be funded out of the savings from not having to build as many plants. The contractors would not have to pay taxes for 5 years and the consumers would get tax credit over the 5 years for 20% of what they saved on oil.

If you think of each house as a "mini plant" that produces the electricity and sends whatever is not used back to the mother plant.

This particular idea helps both with the unemployment problem and reducing our dependence on oil.

#4
THE AMERICAN BANK FOR PUBLIC & PRIVATE SECTOR DEVELOPMENT

Most companies, whether large or small, already have a bank or two. *But there needs to be a bank that focuses on the whole the private sector in its entirety. The whole is greater than the sum of the parts.*

Let me be clear. This is not a government bank or agency. It is an investment bank owned by the private sector for the benefit of the private sector. The Board should be made up of the key players in the private sector. The Secretary of Commerce should be involved but not a member. Its main mission is to arrange long term financing for those projects that are important to its future. Depending on the project there may be a need for PUBLIC /PRIVATE PARTNERSHIPS IN AREAS THAT ARE STRATEGICALLY IMPORTANT TO THE COUNTRY AND THE PRIVATE SECTOR. Clean energy and infrastructure are just two examples. The financings could be both debt and equity, attempting to attract more private equity, hedge fund money and the cash on corporate balance sheets by giving investors adequate returns. Priority projects should be fast tracked by the government. **LET THE COMPANIES BRING THE OVERSEAS CASH HOME AT A 5% RATE IF IT IS INVESTED IN A INFRASTRUCTURE BANK.**

#5
A "QUICK DECISION" CONGRESSIONAL COMMITTEE

Things in Washington just do not get done in the timely way that businesses require. I am sure that you, like me, shake your head at very silly items that are being funded. Many small companies are not hiring people because they may reach the magic number of 50 and in the process have a costly increase in regulatory burden. Somebody has to be empowered to make quick decisions, proper exceptions to unreasonable regulations, and just make good commonsense decisions. Many congressmen agree. The committee would have to be non-partisan and its decisions made public and subject to review.

WHERE ARE THE NEW JOBS?

I can see the jobs. Right now they are sitting in the form of cash on corporations' balance sheets because companies are afraid to invest. More than $2 trillion! Plus another trillion overseas that, if invested in American job creation, should come home "free of taxes." There would be a huge multiplier effect on tax revenues by the jobs created.

Most of the new jobs will come from existing industries. The most important element for job creation is DEMAND. This demand needs to be real not "stimulated". When the government borrows money in forces it into the economy it is stimulating a short lived effect in the economy which most likely will do nothing permanent but increase the debt. The increased debt will worry future investors and decrease the attractiveness of America as a place to do business.

If we lower taxes, and lower the costs of regulation, businesses of all sizes start to develop CONFIDENCE. They have a lower cost of capital and it is easier for their investments to hit their ROI's. They slowly start to add employees who in turn start to spend and create incremental demand. This is how a downward spiraling negative cycle starts to turn and become an upward positive cycle that begins growth.

Many of the new jobs will come from evolving industries that are being forced to change from all sorts of environmental forces.

Where are the jobs? They are on the drawing boards right now all over the country in R & D departments but effectively in "prison."

Here are some of the jobs:

Converting trucks and buses to gas
Natural gas outlets on our highways (Iran's cars run on natural gas!)
Integrate Solar, wind and nuclear into the plan.
Increase domestic drilling until alternative can kick in
Housing & building design and materials
Clinton's building retrofit plan
Exportation of natural gas
Turn housing into a job creator

Innovation Incubator Parks; Science & Mathematics

The promotion of "Entrepreneurship and Innovation" is key to the future of America. It has made us what we are today and it will do so in the future. If we align our efforts we have a better chance to weather ANY STORM, including the one that has just started.

PART III
Let's Be Honest
with Ourselves

A List of Commonsense Questions

- Why do we not have a plan for medicare and social security after all these years?

- Why does the government pay for the prescription drugs of the very wealthy?

- Why don't we have a national energy policy?

- Why is there no plan to fix FANNIE & FREDDIE and restore a functioning secondary market for mortgages?

- After 5 years why is there no exchange for trading credit default swaps that clearly shows everyone's exposure?

- If money in politics is such a big problem why do don't we insist on campaign finance reform?

- Why should really rich people get unemployment, social security and medicare?

- Why is it that year after year we talk about massive waste in government and healthcare? Who are the people responsible for all this waste? Why don't we have a cabinet member to get rid of waste?

- Doesn't ObamaCare need to be streamlined given the deficit? Or because of all the problems and misrepresentations?

- If tort reform is hurting Health Care costs why do we just ignore it? How long do we let the lobbyists rule?

WHAT DID WE LEARN FROM IRAQ & AFGHANISTAN

We did not win nor lose the wars in Afghanistan and Iraq. There were "good things" and "bad things" that happened.

The good things: the total love and admiration for the troops
the death of Osama bin Laden
the death of Sadam Hussein
the elimination of many Al Qaeda leaders
we have not had a subsequent attack within our borders
drones and special forces made a deciding difference

The bad things: never go to war based upon BAD intelligence
nationbuilding should not be our mission
Bin Laden's goal was to hurt our economy... And he did
too many lives lost; too many wounded
Iraq is becoming an ally of Iran
Afghanistan is becoming an ally of the bad part of Pakistan
Al Qaeda has moved to Yemen and Somalia & Africa

From what we learned in Afghanistan and Iraq, we need to have an entire new approach to fighting terrorism.

FIGHTING TERRORISM IS LIKE FIGHTING CANCER

Prevention
Early Detection
Chemotherapy
Radiation & Targeted Surgery
Constant Monitoring

PREVENTION—"Listening"

In my old age I have become a student of listening. Usually, when I am in the middle of an argument, I am formulating my response before the other person gets the words out of their mouth. That is why I say that I do my best listening a day later. To be a good listener requires empathy and a commitment to the communication process. In health it is very important to listen to your body. In fighting terrorism you have to listen to your enemies, and the non- committed who may become your enemy. The world is screaming out at us that we have been arrogant, materialistic and most of all too quick to "pull the trigger."

I am convinced that most people in the world want peace. This is a good thing if we can harness that power. These good people, like most of us, are scared to death of terrorism and nuclear weapons. But there are a small percentage of very evil people in the world who just want to kill us because they have been indoctrinated to believe that we are Satan. If we confuse the good people with the small percentage of truly evil people we will mess it up. Killing innocent people in the name of freedom or democracy is one way to mess it up. The cancer will spread and cause more illness.

There are many things a person can do to increase the odds of not getting cancer. Most of them come down to living a healthy lifestyle. Those of you who do this know you have to work at it—**have a plan.** Do we have a plan to avoid a clash of civilizations? Are we working at it? I do not think so. Just like domestic policy our foreign policy seems to react to one crisis after another.

EARLY DETECTION

If you catch the cancer early your odds go up dramatically.

Key to early detection is testing: *intelligence.* Ours was either wrong or manipulated. In hindsight we dropped the ball after the cold war and lowered our investment in both technology and people (listeners). We need to dramatically increase our investments and controls for the required intelligence. In order to fund these investments we need to reduce other parts of the defense department that are either bureaucratic or oriented to the past.

CHEMOTHERAPY

We have made tremendous strides in the fight against cancer by the development of many drugs that start as experiments and end up by dramatically reducing the incidence of certain cancers. Constant fine tuning and experimentation are essential.

Sanctions, like chemotherapy, kill some good cells with the bad. Evil men let the people suffer but it does seem that sanctions with monitoring were keeping Saddam in check.

RADIATION & TARGETED SURGERY

Radiation is the use of special military operations to "take out" really bad cells or training camps. Targeted surgery is the use of our number one strength in conventional warfare: "Shock and Awe." Going into the war our military was feared as the most powerful in the world. Now the whole world can see how a super power can get stuck in a quagmire that saps its power, economy and reputation. We are not good at, nor should we, occupy other countries. Use overwhelming force very selectively but *get in, get it over, and get out.*

CONSTANT MONITORING

In the circle of life, and the circle of fighting terrorism, we are led back to prevention and early detection—intelligence correctly interpreted with targeted follow-up.

THE ACCOUNTABILITY OF THE PRESS

A free press is essential to a successful democracy. If the government controls the press either directly or indirectly democracy will not work. The press has to have the ability to criticize the government and not fear reprisal.

Unfortunately the press has become "big business." They have to compete for ratings and if they don't get the ratings they go out of business. In order to get the ratings they turned to sensationalism. If they can catch a public official in an embarrassing situation it will get the public's attention and improve their ratings. More and more the press has become part of the entertainment industry. There are radical programs both Republican and Democratic that are vicious and mean-spirited and not a good reflection of us as a nation. Even the main stream press has a biased orientation to one political philosophy or another and it is obvious to the viewer. In a country that is split down the middle all this does is stir up emotions and get in the way of clear thinking.

The people of the press have a tremendous responsibility. They need to ask themselves very seriously whether they are presenting unbiased factual information or are they trying to convince the public of a certain position? Often times this problem is not in an outright lie but that selection of what gets included or excluded in a story or a comment.

PART IV
Becoming a More Spiritual Society

THE BOOMERS' LAST CHANCE

The Ugly American—40 Years Later

In 1965 I won a scholarship from the Paragon Oil Company (now Texaco) to the Georgetown School of Foreign Service. I wrote an essay on the book The Ugly American with great determination to change the image of America in the world. After 40 years in Banking, most of them at Chase Manhattan, it seems that I have hardly succeeded in my quest.

If it is true that the older we get the wiser we get then there is great hope for America as millions of baby boomers become wiser. Think about how much all of these people have learned over the last 40 years. Wisdom is not just knowledge that we acquire, but the thoughtful application of knowledge to produce something better. Now that the boomers have learned that sex, drugs, rock & roll and SUV's did not buy them the happiness for which they were yearning let's see if they can take that knowledge and produce a better result. Let's see if they can divert the path of history from a clash of civilizations and move us to peaceful coexistence.

Fighting latent racism—learning to live together

Keira knows nothing about racism
Will we teach her?
She sees no color
Only friends to play

Keira and friends—"No Racism Here"

A Letter to Carolyn McCarthy re: Guns, Mental Health & Violence

December 22, 2012

Dear Carolyn,

I have not been able to stop thinking about Sandy Hook since it happened. I think it has to do with the children and the helplessness of all the victims. I believe God put you in this situation as you are uniquely prepared to deal with it. The problem is complex and multidimensional. I wanted to help you as you respond to it with a few thoughts they may help shape your plan.

This horrible act of evil did not happen overnight. It has been "brewing" in front of our eyes for many years. It is made up of three distinct but integrated parts: mental health, availability of guns and finally culture. Let me cover each.

Mental Health

*I start with this because I believe it is the fundamental source from where the problem begins. I do not believe we can pass a bill that will solve this problem but there are important steps that can be taken. The challenge is the identification of individuals who need help and then providing it to them... without violating their right to privacy. If we make the argument that their privacy is less important than potential harm to innocent victims I am afraid of politics. Let us start with something much more simple. **I believe we could rapidly establish a national CONFIDENTIAL hotline (1-800-I NEED HELP).** This would be used by both kids and parents who know something is wrong but do not know what to do. This is a start but does not deal with individuals who do not "self-identify."*

*I believe that almost all of the shooters have a pattern that shows early signs of a problem which we as a society have neglected but really do not know what to do. This is where the privacy issue gets tougher. "Unusual behavior" is quite often a signal. But what if it is nothing? Teachers, classmates and friends need to be taught what to do. Professional assessment and counseling is a big part of reducing negative outcomes but a **training program needs to be developed to identify and get treatment for these individuals in a way that protects their civil rights.** The Yale School of Child Studies would be a good partner with other similar organizations.*

Expectations need to be managed with mental health because it will always be an issue. Our challenge is minimize the number and severity of events.

Gun Availability

Far be it for me to advise you on this issue. Your current approach of re-enforcing the 2nd amendment while prohibiting military style assault weapons and magazine clips is the right course. I believe we can win this one.

As you have pointed out we need to get all the states doing what is already required. This involves funding and building the required database. No one should be able to buy any gun without a background check. Guns cannot be allowed to flow into our urban centers. Guns, kids and drugs do not mix. We end up with "kids killing kids."

Culture

This is really composed of 2 parts; first, the debate of using guns to protect our schools and, second, the glorification and permeation of violence in our society. This is our most difficult challenge because it will be the most divisive. That is why I suggest we take "baby steps."

When I first heard about armed guards in school I was repulsed. However, throughout the country, there are many who feel passionately about the need to give the victims a better chance.

The incidents of gun accidents may go up but massacres may go down. I know that if we do this whoever is holding the gun has to be a stable, well trained person, who should be certified annually. After much thought I recommend that the accountability for this decision be given to the states, municipalities and school districts based upon their knowledge of what would best work for their culture. There is a range of options starting with enhanced security and training, to the use of security guards or policeman. Tasers could be considered or dogs. At the end of the day I make this recommendation because the children belong to the parents who live in that local area. They should have the final say. If we try to impose something centrally it will be a quagmire that will only slow us down. Over time we may learn what works best.

The second part of culture is the glorification of violence. It is everywhere: the movies, hit television programs, the nightly news, cable TV, and video games where some of the children spend hours killing bad guys with life like assault weapons. A young man who spends hours a day has to become desensitized to killing. If that young man already suffers from an abusive background you have a recipe for a disaster. What are the baby steps we can take? At a minimum a rating for violent content, training programs, guidelines as to amounts and types of exposures to different age groups. Parents have to play the leading role in this effort.

I truly hope you find some of these thoughts helpful to be integrated with your own. When Christopher was young, about six, one of his friends died suddenly one Christmas, had a flu that led to inflammation of the heart. I never witnessed anything like the shock that came over the neighborhood. People were numb. Multiply that by

28 and you have Sandy Hook. As you know you never recover but you can move on as an individual to grow and develop... or you can crawl into a hole. We need to get the victims to strive for the former, as you did.

I will be praying for you, Joe Biden and Diane Feinstein. I actually could not think of a better team that has the wisdom and background to move us to a better place. I suspect, once again, this is God's work.

Sincerely,
Don Chaffee

WHAT IS PERSONAL ACCOUNTABILITY?

"You know it when you see it"

This sounds like a pretty basic question but it turns out not to be when the system has become so complex with so many countervailing forces that everyone has basically given up on the government ever being able to work. The choice to just leave it up to others was ok when America was the clear leader in the world with nowhere to go but up. Today America is in a place that we can no longer ignore the consequences of not facing our problems, and doing something about them. As I said at the beginning is that the solution to our problems is easier than the politics of our problems. The good news about that statement is that the problems are solvable.

PERSONAL ACCOUNTABILITY
Means
PERSONAL RESPONSIBILITY

Go back to the Michael Jackson lyrics about "looking at the man in the mirror... and asking him to make a change." To be "accountable" for something you have to be "responsible." We need to start realizing that we, as a group, are responsible for where we are as a country. We have, to a great degree, abdicated to individuals who have become professional tenured politicians.

Take a good look in the mirror... and "show up" for accountability, not just for your own political position.

Colin Arrives; NOT SURE WHO IS MORE TIRED

Looks like personal accountability to me.

THE WORK

Jobs—the Economy/THE GOVERNMENT
Financial Stability... THE DEBT
The Tax Code
Less but better Regulation
Our Physical Security/Global Terrorism
Healthcare/Medicare
Social Security
Education
Trade
Project Energy Independence
Immigration
Racism; Learning to live together
Rebuilding our Infrastructure
Protecting the Earth
Fighting Poverty & Hunger
Reducing Violence—Responsible Gun Ownership
Becoming a more Spiritual Society

"Wow that's a lot of Work"

The End

APPENDIX

Some Family Photos

Timmy, Pops & Keira

Peggy & Colin

Keira Anne—first day of school

Timmy makes a friend

Erin Delaney (5 lb 12 oz.)—six weeks early!

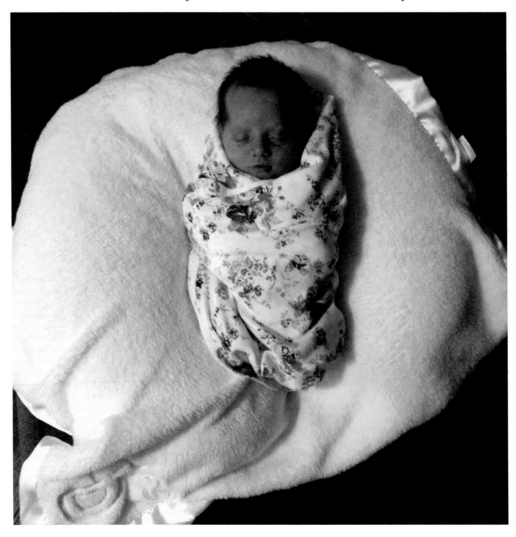

Pops and Ryan

Meg & Tim fall in love

Love...

Pops takes off on next adventure

Pops & Baba Retire

Hold on tight to your children